50 Hearty Soup Recipes for Cold Nights

By: Kelly Johnson

Table of Contents

- Classic Chicken Noodle Soup
- Beef and Barley Stew
- Butternut Squash and Apple Soup
- Creamy Potato Leek Soup
- Slow Cooker Lentil Soup
- Spicy Black Bean Soup
- Mushroom and Wild Rice Soup
- Tomato Basil Soup
- Corn Chowder
- Beef Stroganoff Soup
- French Onion Soup
- White Bean and Kale Soup
- Sweet Potato and Chickpea Soup
- Chicken and Dumplings
- Clam Chowder
- Spicy Roasted Carrot Soup
- Broccoli Cheddar Soup
- Sausage and Kale Soup
- Pumpkin Soup with Coconut Milk
- Split Pea Soup with Ham
- Eggplant Parmesan Soup
- Chicken Tortilla Soup
- Potato and Ham Soup
- Moroccan Harira Soup
- Thai Coconut Chicken Soup
- Cream of Spinach Soup
- Sweet Corn and Chicken Soup
- Cauliflower Cheese Soup
- Italian Wedding Soup
- Goulash Soup
- Smoked Sausage and Potato Soup
- Zuppa Toscana
- Chickpea and Spinach Soup
- Roasted Red Pepper Soup
- Shepherd's Pie Soup

- Kielbasa and Sauerkraut Soup
- Roasted Garlic and Potato Soup
- Tex-Mex Chicken Soup
- Split Pea and Bacon Soup
- Baked Potato Soup
- Creamy Tomato and Spinach Soup
- Vegetable and Bean Soup
- Beef and Cabbage Soup
- Shrimp and Corn Chowder
- Pasta e Fagioli
- Chicken and Rice Soup
- Carrot and Ginger Soup
- Mulligatawny Soup
- Curried Lentil Soup
- New England Fish Chowder

Classic Chicken Noodle Soup

Ingredients:

- 1 tablespoon olive oil
- 1 medium onion, chopped
- 2 carrots, sliced
- 2 celery stalks, sliced
- 3 cloves garlic, minced
- 6 cups chicken broth (or stock)
- 1 bay leaf
- 1 teaspoon dried thyme
- 1 teaspoon dried parsley
- Salt and pepper to taste
- 2 cups cooked chicken, shredded (rotisserie chicken works well)
- 2 cups egg noodles (or any preferred pasta)
- Fresh parsley, chopped (for garnish)

Instructions:

1. **Prepare the Vegetables:**
   - Heat the olive oil in a large pot over medium heat.
   - Add the chopped onion, carrots, and celery. Sauté for 5-7 minutes until the vegetables start to soften.
2. **Add Garlic and Spices:**
   - Add the minced garlic and cook for another minute until fragrant.
   - Stir in the chicken broth, bay leaf, thyme, parsley, salt, and pepper. Bring the mixture to a boil.
3. **Simmer the Soup:**
   - Once boiling, reduce the heat and let the soup simmer for about 20 minutes, allowing the flavors to meld and the vegetables to cook through.
4. **Add Chicken and Noodles:**
   - Stir in the shredded chicken and egg noodles. Cook for an additional 8-10 minutes, or until the noodles are tender.
5. **Serve:**
   - Remove the bay leaf and taste the soup. Adjust seasoning with more salt and pepper, if needed.
   - Ladle the soup into bowls and garnish with fresh parsley.

Beef and Barley Stew

Ingredients:

- 1 tablespoon olive oil
- 1 lb beef stew meat, cubed
- 1 medium onion, chopped
- 2 carrots, sliced
- 2 celery stalks, chopped
- 3 cloves garlic, minced
- 6 cups beef broth
- 1 cup barley
- 2 potatoes, peeled and diced
- 1 bay leaf
- 1 teaspoon dried thyme
- Salt and pepper to taste

Instructions:

1. Heat olive oil in a large pot over medium heat. Add beef and brown on all sides.
2. Add onion, carrots, celery, and garlic. Sauté for 5 minutes.
3. Stir in beef broth, barley, potatoes, bay leaf, thyme, salt, and pepper.
4. Bring to a boil, then reduce heat and simmer for 1–1.5 hours until meat is tender and barley is cooked.
5. Adjust seasoning before serving.

Butternut Squash and Apple Soup

Ingredients:

- 1 tablespoon olive oil
- 1 medium onion, chopped
- 1 butternut squash, peeled, seeded, and cubed
- 2 apples, peeled, cored, and chopped
- 4 cups vegetable broth
- 1/2 teaspoon ground cinnamon
- Salt and pepper to taste
- 1/2 cup heavy cream (optional)

Instructions:

1. Heat olive oil in a large pot. Add onion and sauté for 5 minutes until soft.
2. Add squash, apples, broth, cinnamon, salt, and pepper. Bring to a boil.
3. Reduce heat and simmer for 25–30 minutes, until squash is tender.
4. Blend soup until smooth using an immersion blender or in batches.
5. Stir in cream if desired. Adjust seasoning and serve.

Creamy Potato Leek Soup

Ingredients:

- 2 tablespoons butter
- 2 leeks, cleaned and sliced
- 4 large potatoes, peeled and cubed
- 4 cups vegetable or chicken broth
- 1 cup milk or cream
- Salt and pepper to taste
- Fresh chives, chopped (for garnish)

Instructions:

1. Melt butter in a large pot over medium heat. Add leeks and sauté for 5 minutes.
2. Add potatoes and broth. Bring to a boil, then reduce heat and simmer for 20–25 minutes.
3. Use an immersion blender to blend soup until smooth. Stir in milk or cream.
4. Season with salt and pepper, and garnish with fresh chives.

Slow Cooker Lentil Soup

Ingredients:

- 1 cup dried lentils, rinsed
- 1 onion, chopped
- 2 carrots, chopped
- 2 celery stalks, chopped
- 4 garlic cloves, minced
- 4 cups vegetable broth
- 1 teaspoon ground cumin
- 1 teaspoon dried thyme
- Salt and pepper to taste

Instructions:

1. Place all ingredients into a slow cooker.
2. Cover and cook on low for 7–8 hours or high for 3–4 hours until lentils are tender.
3. Adjust seasoning before serving.

Spicy Black Bean Soup

Ingredients:

- 2 tablespoons olive oil
- 1 onion, chopped
- 2 cloves garlic, minced
- 2 cans (15 oz each) black beans, drained and rinsed
- 4 cups vegetable broth
- 1 can (14.5 oz) diced tomatoes
- 1 teaspoon ground cumin
- 1/2 teaspoon chili powder
- Salt and pepper to taste
- Lime wedges and cilantro for garnish

Instructions:

1. Heat olive oil in a large pot. Add onion and garlic and sauté for 5 minutes.
2. Add beans, broth, tomatoes, cumin, chili powder, salt, and pepper. Bring to a boil.
3. Reduce heat and simmer for 20 minutes.
4. Use an immersion blender to puree the soup for a creamy texture.
5. Garnish with lime wedges and cilantro before serving.

Mushroom and Wild Rice Soup

Ingredients:

- 1 tablespoon olive oil
- 1 onion, chopped
- 3 cups mushrooms, sliced
- 2 cloves garlic, minced
- 6 cups vegetable broth
- 1 cup wild rice, rinsed
- 1/2 cup heavy cream (optional)
- Salt and pepper to taste

Instructions:

1. Heat olive oil in a large pot. Add onion, mushrooms, and garlic. Sauté for 5 minutes.
2. Stir in broth and rice, bring to a boil.
3. Reduce heat and simmer for 40–45 minutes until rice is cooked.
4. Stir in cream if desired. Season with salt and pepper.

Tomato Basil Soup

Ingredients:

- 2 tablespoons olive oil
- 1 onion, chopped
- 4 cups canned tomatoes
- 4 cups vegetable broth
- 1/2 teaspoon dried basil
- 1/2 cup heavy cream (optional)
- Salt and pepper to taste

Instructions:

1. Heat olive oil in a large pot. Add onion and sauté for 5 minutes.
2. Add tomatoes, broth, basil, salt, and pepper. Bring to a boil, then reduce heat and simmer for 15 minutes.
3. Blend the soup until smooth using an immersion blender.
4. Stir in cream if desired. Adjust seasoning before serving.

Corn Chowder

Ingredients:

- 2 tablespoons butter
- 1 onion, chopped
- 2 potatoes, peeled and diced
- 4 cups vegetable broth
- 2 cans (15 oz each) corn kernels, drained
- 1 cup milk or cream
- Salt and pepper to taste
- Fresh thyme or parsley for garnish

Instructions:

1. Heat butter in a large pot. Add onion and sauté for 5 minutes.
2. Add potatoes and broth. Bring to a boil, then reduce heat and simmer for 15–20 minutes.
3. Stir in corn, milk, salt, and pepper. Simmer for an additional 5–10 minutes.
4. Use a potato masher to mash the soup slightly for a creamy texture.
5. Garnish with fresh thyme or parsley before serving.

Beef Stroganoff Soup

Ingredients:

- 1 tablespoon olive oil
- 1 lb beef stew meat, cubed
- 1 medium onion, chopped
- 2 cloves garlic, minced
- 4 cups beef broth
- 2 cups sliced mushrooms
- 1 teaspoon Worcestershire sauce
- 1 teaspoon Dijon mustard
- 1 cup egg noodles
- 1/2 cup sour cream
- 1 tablespoon flour (optional, for thickening)
- Salt and pepper to taste
- Fresh parsley, chopped (for garnish)

Instructions:

1. Heat olive oil in a large pot. Brown the beef stew meat on all sides, then remove and set aside.
2. In the same pot, sauté onion and garlic for 5 minutes. Add mushrooms and cook for an additional 5 minutes.
3. Stir in beef broth, Worcestershire sauce, Dijon mustard, salt, and pepper. Bring to a boil.
4. Add egg noodles and simmer for 10–12 minutes until noodles are tender.
5. Stir in sour cream (and flour for thicker consistency if desired). Adjust seasoning.
6. Garnish with fresh parsley before serving.

French Onion Soup

Ingredients:

- 2 tablespoons butter
- 4 large onions, thinly sliced
- 2 cloves garlic, minced
- 6 cups beef broth
- 1/2 cup dry white wine (optional)
- 1 tablespoon fresh thyme leaves
- 1 bay leaf
- Salt and pepper to taste
- 4 slices French bread, toasted
- 2 cups Gruyère cheese, shredded

Instructions:

1. Melt butter in a large pot over medium heat. Add onions and cook for 20–25 minutes, stirring frequently until caramelized.
2. Add garlic and cook for an additional minute. Stir in broth, wine (if using), thyme, bay leaf, salt, and pepper.
3. Bring to a boil, then reduce to a simmer for 20 minutes. Remove bay leaf.
4. Ladle soup into oven-safe bowls. Place a slice of toasted bread on top of each, and sprinkle with Gruyère cheese.
5. Broil in the oven for 3–5 minutes until cheese is bubbly and golden.

White Bean and Kale Soup

Ingredients:

- 2 tablespoons olive oil
- 1 onion, chopped
- 2 carrots, chopped
- 2 celery stalks, chopped
- 4 garlic cloves, minced
- 6 cups vegetable broth
- 2 cans (15 oz each) white beans, drained and rinsed
- 2 cups chopped kale
- 1 teaspoon dried thyme
- Salt and pepper to taste
- Fresh lemon juice (optional)

Instructions:

1. Heat olive oil in a large pot. Add onion, carrots, and celery, and sauté for 5–7 minutes.
2. Stir in garlic and cook for another minute.
3. Add vegetable broth, beans, thyme, salt, and pepper. Bring to a boil.
4. Reduce heat and simmer for 20 minutes.
5. Stir in kale and simmer for an additional 5 minutes, until tender.
6. Add a squeeze of lemon juice before serving for extra flavor.

Sweet Potato and Chickpea Soup

Ingredients:

- 2 tablespoons olive oil
- 1 onion, chopped
- 2 garlic cloves, minced
- 2 medium sweet potatoes, peeled and cubed
- 1 can (15 oz) chickpeas, drained and rinsed
- 4 cups vegetable broth
- 1 teaspoon ground cumin
- 1/2 teaspoon ground cinnamon
- Salt and pepper to taste
- 1/2 cup coconut milk (optional)

Instructions:

1. Heat olive oil in a large pot. Add onion and garlic, and sauté for 5 minutes until softened.
2. Add sweet potatoes, chickpeas, broth, cumin, cinnamon, salt, and pepper. Bring to a boil.
3. Reduce heat and simmer for 20 minutes, or until sweet potatoes are tender.
4. Use an immersion blender to blend soup until smooth. Stir in coconut milk if desired.
5. Adjust seasoning and serve.

Chicken and Dumplings

Ingredients:

- 2 tablespoons butter
- 1 onion, chopped
- 2 carrots, chopped
- 2 celery stalks, chopped
- 3 cloves garlic, minced
- 4 cups chicken broth
- 2 cups cooked chicken, shredded
- 1 cup frozen peas
- 1 cup milk
- 1 1/2 cups all-purpose flour
- 2 teaspoons baking powder
- 1/2 teaspoon salt
- 1/4 teaspoon ground pepper
- 1/2 cup chopped fresh parsley

Instructions:

1. In a large pot, melt butter over medium heat. Add onion, carrots, celery, and garlic. Sauté for 5–7 minutes.
2. Add chicken broth, cooked chicken, and peas. Bring to a boil.
3. In a separate bowl, mix flour, baking powder, salt, and pepper. Stir in milk to form a thick batter.
4. Drop spoonfuls of batter into the simmering soup. Cover and cook for 15–20 minutes until dumplings are cooked through.
5. Stir in fresh parsley before serving.

Clam Chowder

Ingredients:

- 2 tablespoons butter
- 1 onion, chopped
- 2 celery stalks, chopped
- 2 cloves garlic, minced
- 4 cups clam juice
- 2 cups potatoes, peeled and diced
- 1 can (15 oz) clams, drained and chopped
- 1 cup heavy cream
- 2 tablespoons flour
- Salt and pepper to taste
- Fresh parsley for garnish

Instructions:

1. Melt butter in a large pot. Add onion, celery, and garlic, and sauté for 5 minutes.
2. Stir in clam juice, potatoes, and clams. Bring to a boil, then reduce heat and simmer until potatoes are tender (about 15 minutes).
3. In a small bowl, whisk together flour and heavy cream. Stir into soup and cook for another 5 minutes, until thickened.
4. Season with salt and pepper, and garnish with fresh parsley before serving.

Spicy Roasted Carrot Soup

Ingredients:

- 1 tablespoon olive oil
- 1 lb carrots, peeled and chopped
- 1 onion, chopped
- 2 cloves garlic, minced
- 4 cups vegetable broth
- 1 teaspoon ground cumin
- 1/2 teaspoon chili powder
- Salt and pepper to taste
- 1/2 cup coconut milk (optional)

Instructions:

1. Preheat oven to 400°F (200°C). Toss carrots with olive oil, cumin, chili powder, salt, and pepper. Roast for 25–30 minutes, stirring halfway through.
2. In a large pot, sauté onion and garlic for 5 minutes. Add roasted carrots and vegetable broth.
3. Bring to a boil, then reduce heat and simmer for 15 minutes.
4. Use an immersion blender to blend soup until smooth. Stir in coconut milk if desired.
5. Adjust seasoning before serving.

Broccoli Cheddar Soup

Ingredients:

- 2 tablespoons butter
- 1 onion, chopped
- 2 cloves garlic, minced
- 4 cups broccoli florets
- 4 cups vegetable broth
- 1 cup milk
- 2 cups shredded cheddar cheese
- Salt and pepper to taste

Instructions:

1. Melt butter in a large pot. Add onion and garlic, and sauté for 5 minutes.
2. Add broccoli and broth, and bring to a boil. Reduce heat and simmer for 15–20 minutes until broccoli is tender.
3. Use an immersion blender to blend soup until smooth or leave it chunky.
4. Stir in milk and cheddar cheese until the cheese is melted. Season with salt and pepper.
5. Serve hot with extra cheese if desired.

Sausage and Kale Soup

Ingredients:

- 1 tablespoon olive oil
- 1 lb Italian sausage (mild or spicy), casings removed
- 1 onion, chopped
- 2 cloves garlic, minced
- 4 cups chicken broth
- 2 cups kale, chopped
- 2 large potatoes, peeled and diced
- 1 teaspoon dried oregano
- Salt and pepper to taste
- 1 cup heavy cream (optional)

Instructions:

1. Heat olive oil in a large pot. Add sausage and cook, breaking it apart, until browned.
2. Add onion and garlic, cooking for 5 minutes until softened.
3. Stir in chicken broth, potatoes, oregano, salt, and pepper. Bring to a boil.
4. Reduce heat and simmer for 20 minutes or until potatoes are tender.
5. Stir in kale and cook for an additional 5 minutes.
6. For a creamier soup, add heavy cream and adjust seasoning before serving.

Pumpkin Soup with Coconut Milk

Ingredients:

- 2 tablespoons olive oil
- 1 onion, chopped
- 2 cloves garlic, minced
- 4 cups pumpkin puree
- 2 cups vegetable broth
- 1 can (15 oz) coconut milk
- 1 teaspoon ground cinnamon
- 1/2 teaspoon ground ginger
- Salt and pepper to taste

Instructions:

1. Heat olive oil in a large pot. Add onion and garlic, sautéing for 5 minutes until softened.
2. Stir in pumpkin puree, vegetable broth, cinnamon, ginger, salt, and pepper.
3. Bring to a boil, then reduce to a simmer for 15 minutes.
4. Stir in coconut milk and simmer for another 5 minutes.
5. Blend until smooth using an immersion blender or regular blender, then adjust seasoning before serving.

Split Pea Soup with Ham

Ingredients:

- 2 tablespoons olive oil
- 1 onion, chopped
- 2 cloves garlic, minced
- 2 cups dried split peas, rinsed
- 1 ham bone or 2 cups ham, cubed
- 6 cups chicken broth
- 1 carrot, chopped
- 1 celery stalk, chopped
- 1 teaspoon dried thyme
- Salt and pepper to taste

Instructions:

1. Heat olive oil in a large pot. Add onion and garlic, cooking for 5 minutes until softened.
2. Add split peas, ham bone (or cubed ham), chicken broth, carrot, celery, thyme, salt, and pepper. Bring to a boil.
3. Reduce heat and simmer for 1–1.5 hours, stirring occasionally, until the peas are tender and the soup thickens.
4. Remove ham bone and discard the bone, shredding any remaining meat into the soup.
5. Adjust seasoning and serve.

Eggplant Parmesan Soup

Ingredients:

- 2 tablespoons olive oil
- 1 onion, chopped
- 2 cloves garlic, minced
- 2 eggplants, peeled and diced
- 4 cups vegetable broth
- 1 can (14 oz) diced tomatoes
- 1 teaspoon dried basil
- 1 teaspoon dried oregano
- Salt and pepper to taste
- 1 cup shredded mozzarella cheese
- 1/2 cup grated Parmesan cheese

Instructions:

1. Heat olive oil in a large pot. Add onion and garlic, sautéing for 5 minutes until softened.
2. Stir in eggplant, vegetable broth, diced tomatoes, basil, oregano, salt, and pepper.
3. Bring to a boil, then reduce heat and simmer for 30 minutes, until the eggplant is tender.
4. Use an immersion blender to puree the soup, leaving some texture if desired.
5. Stir in mozzarella and Parmesan cheeses, allowing them to melt before serving.

Chicken Tortilla Soup

Ingredients:

- 1 tablespoon olive oil
- 1 lb chicken breast, cooked and shredded
- 1 onion, chopped
- 2 cloves garlic, minced
- 1 can (14 oz) diced tomatoes
- 4 cups chicken broth
- 1 teaspoon ground cumin
- 1 teaspoon chili powder
- 1/2 teaspoon smoked paprika
- 1/2 cup corn kernels (fresh or frozen)
- Salt and pepper to taste
- Tortilla strips, for garnish
- Fresh cilantro, for garnish
- Shredded cheddar cheese, for garnish
- Sour cream, for garnish

Instructions:

1. Heat olive oil in a large pot. Add onion and garlic, cooking for 5 minutes until softened.
2. Stir in diced tomatoes, chicken broth, cumin, chili powder, smoked paprika, salt, and pepper. Bring to a boil.
3. Reduce heat and simmer for 10–15 minutes to allow flavors to meld.
4. Add shredded chicken and corn, cooking for an additional 5 minutes.
5. Serve topped with tortilla strips, fresh cilantro, shredded cheese, and a dollop of sour cream.

Potato and Ham Soup

Ingredients:

- 2 tablespoons butter
- 1 onion, chopped
- 2 cloves garlic, minced
- 4 cups potatoes, peeled and diced
- 2 cups ham, cubed
- 4 cups chicken broth
- 1 cup milk or heavy cream
- Salt and pepper to taste
- Fresh parsley, chopped for garnish

Instructions:

1. Melt butter in a large pot. Add onion and garlic, sautéing for 5 minutes until softened.
2. Stir in potatoes, ham, chicken broth, salt, and pepper. Bring to a boil.
3. Reduce heat and simmer for 20–25 minutes until potatoes are tender.
4. Stir in milk or heavy cream, cooking for an additional 5 minutes.
5. Adjust seasoning and serve garnished with fresh parsley.

Moroccan Harira Soup

Ingredients:

- 2 tablespoons olive oil
- 1 onion, chopped
- 2 cloves garlic, minced
- 1 carrot, chopped
- 2 celery stalks, chopped
- 1 can (14 oz) diced tomatoes
- 4 cups vegetable broth
- 1 can (15 oz) chickpeas, drained and rinsed
- 1/2 cup lentils, rinsed
- 1 teaspoon ground cumin
- 1 teaspoon ground coriander
- 1/2 teaspoon ground cinnamon
- 1/4 teaspoon ground turmeric
- Salt and pepper to taste
- Fresh cilantro, chopped for garnish
- Fresh lemon juice (optional)

Instructions:

1. Heat olive oil in a large pot. Add onion, garlic, carrot, and celery, cooking for 5 minutes until softened.
2. Stir in diced tomatoes, vegetable broth, chickpeas, lentils, cumin, coriander, cinnamon, turmeric, salt, and pepper. Bring to a boil.
3. Reduce heat and simmer for 30–40 minutes until lentils are tender.
4. Adjust seasoning with salt, pepper, and fresh lemon juice before serving. Garnish with cilantro.

Thai Coconut Chicken Soup

Ingredients:

- 1 tablespoon olive oil
- 1 lb chicken breast, thinly sliced
- 1 onion, chopped
- 2 cloves garlic, minced
- 1 can (14 oz) coconut milk
- 4 cups chicken broth
- 1 tablespoon grated ginger
- 2 tablespoons fish sauce
- 1 teaspoon lime zest
- 1 tablespoon lime juice
- 1/2 teaspoon chili flakes (optional)
- Fresh cilantro, chopped for garnish

Instructions:

1. Heat olive oil in a large pot. Add chicken breast, onion, and garlic, cooking until the chicken is browned.
2. Stir in coconut milk, chicken broth, ginger, fish sauce, lime zest, and chili flakes. Bring to a boil.
3. Reduce heat and simmer for 15 minutes to allow flavors to meld.
4. Stir in lime juice and adjust seasoning. Garnish with fresh cilantro before serving.

Cream of Spinach Soup

Ingredients:

- 2 tablespoons butter
- 1 onion, chopped
- 2 cloves garlic, minced
- 6 cups fresh spinach
- 4 cups vegetable broth
- 1 cup heavy cream
- 1 teaspoon ground nutmeg
- Salt and pepper to taste

Instructions:

1. Melt butter in a large pot. Add onion and garlic, sautéing for 5 minutes until softened.
2. Stir in spinach and cook until wilted, about 3–5 minutes.
3. Add vegetable broth, nutmeg, salt, and pepper, and bring to a boil.
4. Reduce heat and simmer for 10–15 minutes. Use an immersion blender to blend until smooth.
5. Stir in heavy cream and adjust seasoning before serving.

Sweet Corn and Chicken Soup

Ingredients:

- 1 tablespoon olive oil
- 1 lb chicken breast, cooked and shredded
- 1 onion, chopped
- 2 cloves garlic, minced
- 4 cups chicken broth
- 2 cups frozen corn kernels
- 1 cup carrots, diced
- 1 teaspoon ground cumin
- 1 teaspoon chili powder
- Salt and pepper to taste
- Fresh cilantro, chopped for garnish

Instructions:

1. Heat olive oil in a large pot. Add onion and garlic, cooking for 5 minutes until softened.
2. Stir in chicken broth, chicken, corn, carrots, cumin, chili powder, salt, and pepper. Bring to a boil.
3. Reduce heat and simmer for 15–20 minutes until carrots are tender.
4. Adjust seasoning and serve garnished with fresh cilantro.

Cauliflower Cheese Soup

Ingredients:

- 2 tablespoons butter
- 1 onion, chopped
- 2 cloves garlic, minced
- 1 head cauliflower, chopped into florets
- 4 cups vegetable broth
- 1 cup shredded cheddar cheese
- 1/2 cup heavy cream
- Salt and pepper to taste

Instructions:

1. Melt butter in a large pot. Add onion and garlic, sautéing for 5 minutes until softened.
2. Stir in cauliflower and vegetable broth, bringing to a boil.
3. Reduce heat and simmer for 20–25 minutes, until cauliflower is tender.
4. Use an immersion blender to puree the soup until smooth.
5. Stir in shredded cheddar cheese and heavy cream, then adjust seasoning before serving.

Italian Wedding Soup

Ingredients:

- 2 tablespoons olive oil
- 1 lb ground beef
- 1/2 cup breadcrumbs
- 1/4 cup grated Parmesan cheese
- 1 egg
- 2 teaspoons dried Italian seasoning
- 6 cups chicken broth
- 1 cup carrots, sliced
- 1 cup spinach, chopped
- 1/2 cup acini di pepe pasta
- Salt and pepper to taste

Instructions:

1. Preheat the oven to 375°F (190°C). In a bowl, mix ground beef, breadcrumbs, Parmesan, egg, Italian seasoning, salt, and pepper. Roll the mixture into small meatballs and bake for 15–20 minutes.
2. Heat olive oil in a large pot, then add chicken broth, carrots, and spinach. Bring to a boil.
3. Add cooked meatballs and pasta, cooking for an additional 10 minutes until the pasta is tender.
4. Adjust seasoning and serve.

Goulash Soup

Ingredients:

- 2 tablespoons olive oil
- 1 lb beef stew meat, cubed
- 1 onion, chopped
- 2 cloves garlic, minced
- 1 tablespoon paprika
- 4 cups beef broth
- 1 can (14 oz) diced tomatoes
- 1 cup potatoes, diced
- 1 cup bell pepper, chopped
- Salt and pepper to taste

Instructions:

1. Heat olive oil in a large pot. Brown the beef stew meat, then add onion and garlic, cooking until softened.
2. Stir in paprika, beef broth, diced tomatoes, potatoes, bell pepper, salt, and pepper. Bring to a boil.
3. Reduce heat and simmer for 30–40 minutes until potatoes are tender.
4. Adjust seasoning and serve.

Smoked Sausage and Potato Soup

Ingredients:

- 2 tablespoons olive oil
- 1 lb smoked sausage, sliced
- 1 onion, chopped
- 2 cloves garlic, minced
- 4 cups chicken broth
- 4 cups potatoes, peeled and diced
- 1 cup heavy cream
- 1 teaspoon dried thyme
- Salt and pepper to taste

Instructions:

1. Heat olive oil in a large pot. Add smoked sausage, onion, and garlic, cooking until browned.
2. Stir in chicken broth, potatoes, thyme, salt, and pepper. Bring to a boil.
3. Reduce heat and simmer for 20 minutes, until potatoes are tender.
4. Stir in heavy cream and cook for another 5 minutes before serving.

Zuppa Toscana

Ingredients:

- 1 tablespoon olive oil
- 1 lb Italian sausage, casings removed
- 1 onion, chopped
- 2 cloves garlic, minced
- 4 cups chicken broth
- 4 cups kale, chopped
- 3 potatoes, peeled and sliced
- 1 cup heavy cream
- Salt and pepper to taste

Instructions:

1. Heat olive oil in a large pot. Add sausage, onion, and garlic, cooking until browned.
2. Stir in chicken broth, kale, and potatoes, bringing to a boil.
3. Reduce heat and simmer for 20–25 minutes, until potatoes are tender.
4. Stir in heavy cream, adjust seasoning, and serve.

Chickpea and Spinach Soup

Ingredients:

- 2 tablespoons olive oil
- 1 onion, chopped
- 2 cloves garlic, minced
- 2 cans (15 oz each) chickpeas, drained and rinsed
- 4 cups vegetable broth
- 2 cups spinach, chopped
- 1 teaspoon ground cumin
- Salt and pepper to taste
- Fresh lemon juice, for garnish

Instructions:

1. Heat olive oil in a large pot. Add onion and garlic, cooking for 5 minutes until softened.
2. Stir in chickpeas, vegetable broth, cumin, salt, and pepper. Bring to a boil.
3. Reduce heat and simmer for 10 minutes, then stir in spinach and cook for another 5 minutes.
4. Adjust seasoning and serve with a squeeze of fresh lemon juice.

Roasted Red Pepper Soup

Ingredients:

- 2 tablespoons olive oil
- 2 red bell peppers, roasted and peeled
- 1 onion, chopped
- 2 cloves garlic, minced
- 4 cups vegetable broth
- 1 cup heavy cream
- Salt and pepper to taste

Instructions:

1. Heat olive oil in a large pot. Add onion and garlic, sautéing for 5 minutes until softened.
2. Stir in roasted red peppers and vegetable broth, bringing to a boil.
3. Reduce heat and simmer for 10 minutes, then blend until smooth using an immersion blender.
4. Stir in heavy cream and adjust seasoning before serving.

Shepherd's Pie Soup

Ingredients:

- 2 tablespoons olive oil
- 1 lb ground lamb or beef
- 1 onion, chopped
- 2 cloves garlic, minced
- 4 cups beef broth
- 2 cups potatoes, peeled and diced
- 1 cup frozen peas
- 1 cup carrots, chopped
- 1 teaspoon dried thyme
- Salt and pepper to taste

Instructions:

1. Heat olive oil in a large pot. Add ground lamb or beef, onion, and garlic, cooking until browned.
2. Stir in beef broth, potatoes, peas, carrots, thyme, salt, and pepper. Bring to a boil.
3. Reduce heat and simmer for 30 minutes, until potatoes are tender.
4. Adjust seasoning and serve, optionally topping with mashed potatoes.

Kielbasa and Sauerkraut Soup

Ingredients:

- 2 tablespoons olive oil
- 1 lb kielbasa, sliced
- 1 onion, chopped
- 2 cloves garlic, minced
- 4 cups chicken broth
- 1 can (15 oz) sauerkraut, drained and rinsed
- 2 cups potatoes, diced
- 1 cup carrots, chopped
- 1 teaspoon caraway seeds (optional)
- Salt and pepper to taste

Instructions:

1. Heat olive oil in a large pot. Add kielbasa, onion, and garlic, cooking until browned and softened.
2. Stir in chicken broth, sauerkraut, potatoes, carrots, caraway seeds (if using), salt, and pepper. Bring to a boil.
3. Reduce heat and simmer for 30 minutes, until potatoes are tender.
4. Adjust seasoning and serve.

Roasted Garlic and Potato Soup

Ingredients:

- 2 heads garlic, roasted (see instructions below)
- 2 tablespoons olive oil
- 1 onion, chopped
- 4 cups chicken broth
- 4 cups potatoes, peeled and diced
- 1 cup heavy cream
- Salt and pepper to taste
- Fresh thyme for garnish

Instructions:

1. To roast the garlic, cut the tops off the garlic heads, drizzle with olive oil, and wrap in foil. Roast at 400°F (200°C) for 30–40 minutes, until soft.
2. In a large pot, heat olive oil and sauté onion until softened.
3. Squeeze the roasted garlic into the pot, then stir in chicken broth and potatoes. Bring to a boil.
4. Reduce heat and simmer for 20–25 minutes until potatoes are tender.
5. Use an immersion blender to puree the soup. Stir in heavy cream, adjust seasoning, and garnish with fresh thyme.

Tex-Mex Chicken Soup

Ingredients:

- 1 tablespoon olive oil
- 1 lb chicken breast, cooked and shredded
- 1 onion, chopped
- 2 cloves garlic, minced
- 1 can (15 oz) diced tomatoes with green chilies
- 4 cups chicken broth
- 1 can (15 oz) corn kernels, drained
- 1 teaspoon ground cumin
- 1 teaspoon chili powder
- Salt and pepper to taste
- Fresh cilantro for garnish
- Lime wedges for serving

Instructions:

1. Heat olive oil in a large pot. Add onion and garlic, cooking until softened.
2. Stir in diced tomatoes, chicken broth, corn, shredded chicken, cumin, chili powder, salt, and pepper. Bring to a boil.
3. Reduce heat and simmer for 15 minutes.
4. Adjust seasoning, serve with fresh cilantro, and squeeze lime juice on top.

Split Pea and Bacon Soup

Ingredients:

- 2 tablespoons olive oil
- 4 slices bacon, chopped
- 1 onion, chopped
- 2 cloves garlic, minced
- 2 cups split peas, rinsed
- 4 cups vegetable or chicken broth
- 2 carrots, chopped
- 2 celery stalks, chopped
- 1 teaspoon dried thyme
- Salt and pepper to taste

Instructions:

1. Heat olive oil in a large pot. Add bacon and cook until crispy.
2. Remove bacon and set aside. Add onion and garlic to the pot, cooking until softened.
3. Stir in split peas, broth, carrots, celery, thyme, salt, and pepper. Bring to a boil.
4. Reduce heat and simmer for 40–45 minutes, until split peas are tender.
5. Garnish with bacon and adjust seasoning before serving.

Baked Potato Soup

Ingredients:

- 2 tablespoons olive oil
- 1 onion, chopped
- 4 cups chicken broth
- 4 large russet potatoes, baked and diced
- 1 cup heavy cream
- 1 cup shredded cheddar cheese
- 1/2 cup sour cream
- Salt and pepper to taste
- Green onions for garnish
- Crispy bacon, crumbled for garnish

Instructions:

1. Heat olive oil in a large pot. Add onion, cooking for 5 minutes until softened.
2. Stir in chicken broth, baked potatoes, heavy cream, and salt and pepper. Bring to a boil.
3. Reduce heat and simmer for 10 minutes. Use a potato masher to mash some of the potatoes.
4. Stir in shredded cheese and sour cream. Garnish with green onions and crumbled bacon before serving.

Creamy Tomato and Spinach Soup

Ingredients:

- 2 tablespoons olive oil
- 1 onion, chopped
- 2 cloves garlic, minced
- 2 cans (14 oz each) diced tomatoes
- 4 cups vegetable broth
- 2 cups fresh spinach, chopped
- 1 teaspoon dried basil
- 1 cup heavy cream
- Salt and pepper to taste

Instructions:

1. Heat olive oil in a large pot. Add onion and garlic, cooking until softened.
2. Stir in diced tomatoes, vegetable broth, spinach, basil, salt, and pepper. Bring to a boil.
3. Reduce heat and simmer for 15 minutes. Use an immersion blender to puree the soup until smooth.
4. Stir in heavy cream and adjust seasoning before serving.

Vegetable and Bean Soup

Ingredients:

- 2 tablespoons olive oil
- 1 onion, chopped
- 2 cloves garlic, minced
- 2 carrots, chopped
- 2 celery stalks, chopped
- 2 cups vegetable broth
- 1 can (15 oz) white beans, drained and rinsed
- 1 can (15 oz) diced tomatoes
- 1 cup zucchini, chopped
- 1 cup green beans, chopped
- 1 teaspoon dried basil
- Salt and pepper to taste

Instructions:

1. Heat olive oil in a large pot. Add onion and garlic, cooking until softened.
2. Stir in carrots, celery, vegetable broth, white beans, tomatoes, zucchini, green beans, basil, salt, and pepper. Bring to a boil.
3. Reduce heat and simmer for 25–30 minutes, until vegetables are tender.
4. Adjust seasoning and serve.

Beef and Cabbage Soup

Ingredients:

- 2 tablespoons olive oil
- 1 lb ground beef
- 1 onion, chopped
- 2 cloves garlic, minced
- 4 cups beef broth
- 4 cups cabbage, shredded
- 2 cups carrots, chopped
- 2 potatoes, diced
- 1 teaspoon dried thyme
- Salt and pepper to taste

Instructions:

1. Heat olive oil in a large pot. Add ground beef, onion, and garlic, cooking until browned.
2. Stir in beef broth, cabbage, carrots, potatoes, thyme, salt, and pepper. Bring to a boil.
3. Reduce heat and simmer for 30 minutes, until potatoes and vegetables are tender.
4. Adjust seasoning and serve.

Shrimp and Corn Chowder

Ingredients:

- 2 tablespoons olive oil
- 1 lb shrimp, peeled and deveined
- 1 onion, chopped
- 2 cloves garlic, minced
- 4 cups chicken or seafood broth
- 2 cups corn kernels (fresh or frozen)
- 2 cups potatoes, diced
- 1 teaspoon paprika
- 1 cup heavy cream
- Salt and pepper to taste
- Fresh parsley for garnish

Instructions:

1. Heat olive oil in a large pot. Add shrimp, cooking until pink, then set aside.
2. In the same pot, add onion and garlic, cooking until softened.
3. Stir in broth, corn, potatoes, paprika, salt, and pepper. Bring to a boil.
4. Reduce heat and simmer for 20 minutes, until potatoes are tender.
5. Stir in heavy cream, then return shrimp to the pot. Adjust seasoning and garnish with parsley before serving.

Pasta e Fagioli

Ingredients:

- 2 tablespoons olive oil
- 1 onion, chopped
- 2 cloves garlic, minced
- 2 carrots, chopped
- 2 celery stalks, chopped
- 1 can (15 oz) cannellini beans, drained and rinsed
- 1 can (14 oz) diced tomatoes
- 4 cups vegetable or chicken broth
- 1 cup small pasta (like ditalini or elbow macaroni)
- 1 teaspoon dried oregano
- Salt and pepper to taste
- Fresh basil or parsley for garnish
- Grated Parmesan cheese for serving

Instructions:

1. Heat olive oil in a large pot. Add onion, garlic, carrots, and celery, cooking until softened.
2. Stir in beans, diced tomatoes, broth, pasta, oregano, salt, and pepper. Bring to a boil.
3. Reduce heat and simmer for 15-20 minutes, until the pasta is tender.
4. Garnish with fresh herbs and grated Parmesan cheese before serving.

Chicken and Rice Soup

Ingredients:

- 2 tablespoons olive oil
- 1 onion, chopped
- 2 cloves garlic, minced
- 2 carrots, chopped
- 2 celery stalks, chopped
- 4 cups chicken broth
- 1 cup cooked chicken, shredded
- 1/2 cup rice
- 1 teaspoon dried thyme
- Salt and pepper to taste
- Fresh parsley for garnish

Instructions:

1. Heat olive oil in a large pot. Add onion, garlic, carrots, and celery, cooking until softened.
2. Stir in chicken broth, chicken, rice, thyme, salt, and pepper. Bring to a boil.
3. Reduce heat and simmer for 15-20 minutes, until the rice is tender.
4. Garnish with fresh parsley before serving.

Carrot and Ginger Soup

Ingredients:

- 2 tablespoons olive oil
- 1 onion, chopped
- 2 cloves garlic, minced
- 4 cups carrots, peeled and chopped
- 1-inch piece fresh ginger, peeled and grated
- 4 cups vegetable or chicken broth
- Salt and pepper to taste
- Fresh parsley for garnish

Instructions:

1. Heat olive oil in a large pot. Add onion and garlic, cooking until softened.
2. Stir in carrots and ginger, cooking for 2-3 minutes.
3. Add broth, salt, and pepper. Bring to a boil.
4. Reduce heat and simmer for 20-25 minutes, until the carrots are tender.
5. Use an immersion blender to puree the soup until smooth. Garnish with fresh parsley before serving.

Mulligatawny Soup

Ingredients:

- 2 tablespoons olive oil
- 1 onion, chopped
- 2 cloves garlic, minced
- 1 tablespoon curry powder
- 1 teaspoon ground ginger
- 4 cups chicken broth
- 1 cup cooked chicken, shredded
- 1 cup apples, peeled and chopped
- 1/2 cup rice
- 1 can (14 oz) coconut milk
- Salt and pepper to taste
- Fresh cilantro for garnish

Instructions:

1. Heat olive oil in a large pot. Add onion and garlic, cooking until softened.
2. Stir in curry powder and ground ginger, cooking for 1 minute until fragrant.
3. Add chicken broth, chicken, apples, rice, and coconut milk. Bring to a boil.
4. Reduce heat and simmer for 20-25 minutes, until the rice is tender.
5. Adjust seasoning with salt and pepper. Garnish with fresh cilantro before serving.

Curried Lentil Soup

Ingredients:

- 2 tablespoons olive oil
- 1 onion, chopped
- 2 cloves garlic, minced
- 1 tablespoon curry powder
- 1 cup red lentils, rinsed
- 4 cups vegetable broth
- 1 can (14 oz) diced tomatoes
- 1 teaspoon ground turmeric
- Salt and pepper to taste
- Fresh cilantro for garnish

Instructions:

1. Heat olive oil in a large pot. Add onion and garlic, cooking until softened.
2. Stir in curry powder and turmeric, cooking for 1 minute until fragrant.
3. Add lentils, broth, and diced tomatoes. Bring to a boil.
4. Reduce heat and simmer for 25-30 minutes, until the lentils are tender.
5. Adjust seasoning with salt and pepper. Garnish with fresh cilantro before serving.

New England Fish Chowder

Ingredients:

- 2 tablespoons butter
- 1 onion, chopped
- 2 cloves garlic, minced
- 4 cups fish stock or chicken broth
- 2 cups potatoes, peeled and diced
- 1 cup corn kernels (fresh or frozen)
- 1 lb white fish fillets (like cod or haddock), cut into chunks
- 1 cup heavy cream
- Salt and pepper to taste
- Fresh parsley for garnish

Instructions:

1. Melt butter in a large pot. Add onion and garlic, cooking until softened.
2. Stir in fish stock, potatoes, and corn. Bring to a boil.
3. Reduce heat and simmer for 15-20 minutes, until potatoes are tender.
4. Add the fish fillets and cook for another 5-7 minutes until the fish is cooked through.
5. Stir in heavy cream, salt, and pepper. Garnish with fresh parsley before serving.

www.ingramcontent.com/pod-product-compliance
Lightning Source LLC
LaVergne TN
LVHW081338060526
838201LV00055B/2729